stewardship

Simply Generous
Published by Stewardship
1 Lamb's Passage
London
EC1Y 8AB

stewardship.org.uk

enquiries@stewardship.org.uk

ISBN 978-1-5262-0624-4

CONTENTS

6 Foreword

8 Introduction: Life itself…

16 Generosity's first steps

22 Generosity can be risky (Thank God)

28 Generosity thrives when planned

34 Generosity costs, but it also transforms

40 Generosity is infectious

48 Generosity builds character

54 Generosity is messy, but it clears things up

60 Generosity will change you more than you think

66 Generosity's journey leads us to new destinations

72 Epilogue: What next?

FOREWORD

We talk about generosity a lot at Stewardship. All the time, in fact. But even by our standards, the conversations have lasted longer and voices grown louder over the last four years. For while the news on our screens has been dominated by terror and fear, we've seen a rise in the number of stories of people choosing to embrace generosity and live with eyes, hands and homes open.

Not that generosity is anything new. History has handed down plenty of stories of remarkable courage and selflessness. But generosity never gets old, and there's something uniquely wonderful about seeing your peers and friends thrive in life. That's why we find these stories that are playing out around us to be truly captivating.

You'll inch open the door to see what a life transformed by generosity can look like.

The more we've talked about the wonderful choices that everyday Christians are making, the more we realised that we wanted to share them in print. So, over the last four years, we've made a point of meeting up with them, capturing their stories and thinking about what essential and different lessons each one can teach us about how to live a more generous life.

Because generosity is something that can – and should – be taught.

Not that we're trying to make it complicated, academic or abstract. Far from it. We want to remind people of how powerful it is, how innate, and how simple.

That's why we hope that, as you read through these pages, you'll inch open the door to see what a life transformed by generosity can look like. We hope that you'll see the invitation that generosity offers, that you'll get a sense of what's in store for everyone who takes a risk and makes the choice.

Most of all, we hope that on finishing the book you'll find yourself inspired, equipped and ready to take a new risk with all that you've been given.

Michael O'Neill

INTRODUCTION: LIFE ITSELF...

God made us in his image

'Let us make human beings in our image, make them reflecting our nature.'
(Genesis 1:27, The Message)

God made us to live in relationship with him as well as to be in relationship with others.

The Trinity itself – Father, Son and Spirit – is a perfect picture of generosity, as John 3:34–36 makes clear: 'For the one whom God has sent speaks the words of God, for God gives the Spirit without limit. The Father loves the Son and has placed everything in his hands. Whoever believes in the Son has eternal life, but whoever rejects the Son will not see life, for God's wrath remains on them.'

We are designed similarly to receive and give in a perpetual cycle of generosity. But, despite generosity being part of our factory settings, it is not an involuntary action; we don't *have* to give. We can choose to leave it dormant – keeping our arms metaphorically folded. Or we can choose to activate it, by opening our arms and receiving

Why receive first?

You may wonder why the cycle of generosity starts with receiving.

When Paul writes 'Thanks be to God for his indescribable gift!' (2 Corinthians 9:15) he reminds us that the source of grace and generosity is God himself. Generosity begins with God's gift to us. It all starts with our hands held open to the kind of generosity which can transform the extreme poverty of the Macedonian churches into overflowing joy.

Joy has a key role to play within generosity. Sometimes – often, in fact – we will find that being generous leaves us feeling good, but that sense of happiness is not the primary reason for giving. We give because we are grateful to God for his own gift to us. Generosity thrives best when it is an expression of the joy that God has sparked in our lives.

If we lose sight of the source, of the 'indescribable gift', our view of generosity becomes restricted, a pale imitation of the technicolour generosity of the Macedonian churches. If giving becomes a chore, driven by duty or guilt, the whole thing becomes lifeless and dull. There is no joy.

When Paul writes to the church in Philippi he repeats the word 'rejoice' several times. He understands that joy and generosity cannot be separated.

Truly generous?

What does it look like to live a truly generous life? Generosity has been evident since the dawn of creation, but something significant happened 2000 years ago when God came and lived among us. Jesus walked the land, from village to city, from home to well, walking and working in the unforced rhythms of grace. He was generous with his gifts of healing, generous with his forgiveness of sinners, generous in his invitation to others to follow him. And he knew how to receive too: praise, food, adoration, clothing and shelter. Jesus lived both as a receiver, from the moment of his birth, and as a giver, until he performed his last miracle – generous forgiveness for all from a cross. Jesus' life – and death – became the most perfect articulation of generosity in action. He lived and breathed it.

Jesus spoke of coming to earth so 'that they may have life, and have it abundantly' (John 10:10, NRSV). Jesus is our model for that abundant, generous life both in the parables he used for teaching and in the way in which he lived and moved among people. One was not distinct from the other.

For example, when an expert in the Law asked Jesus what to do in order to inherit eternal life, Jesus went on to tell the story of the Samaritan on the road to Jericho (Luke10:25–37). The parable gives us a perfect template for generosity, shown through a life in which love overcomes fear; from the moment the Samaritan sees the man's predicament, he puts aside his own agenda and goes the extra mile. It's the kind of generosity which is very practical but is also rooted in loving God 'with all your heart and with all your soul and with all your strength' (v. 27).

Generosity is not something that happens to us, and It is not something that will overrule us. Our part in the story of generosity only begins when we say 'yes'.

The rich man in Matthew's Gospel asks the same question, 'Teacher, what good thing must I do to get eternal life?' (Matthew 19:16). Jesus tells him to keep the commandments and love his neighbour, but the man is still confused. So Jesus spells it out for him; sell his possessions, embrace generosity and say 'yes' to Jesus' offer of a relationship with him. The man declines.

A generous paradox

Here is the paradox of generosity. Despite its magnificent power and incredible potential, we can say no to it. It is possible to go through life with our backs turned to generosity. We can choose to allow it to enter our lives by the smallest degree, or we can surrender to it completely. Generosity is not something that happens to us, and it is not something that will overrule us. Our part in the story of generosity only begins when we say 'yes'.

For some of us, like the rich man in Matthew, there are just too many reasons to say 'no'.

True generosity

By way of contrast, let's consider another real-life example:

'As he looked up, Jesus saw the rich putting their gifts into the temple treasury. He also saw a poor widow put in two very small copper coins. "I tell you the truth," he said, "this poor widow has put in more than all the others. All these people gave their gifts out of their wealth; but she out of her poverty put in all she had to live on."'
(Luke 21:1–4)

Jesus is spending the last week of his life teaching in the temple when his eye is drawn to the activity around the treasury. He spots the rich giving ostentatiously and spies the widow giving just a fraction. In today's terms it probably would equate to the cost of her main meal for the day, but for a widow there is no safety net; she gives knowing it is all she has. Her generosity, commitment and passion move Jesus, and her generous gift foreshadows his coming passion, his indescribable gift of grace and salvation for all of us.

Her generosity is also a complete contrast to the measured generosity of some other rich givers. Like the Macedonian churches, she gives out of her poverty and unlike the rich young man she does not hesitate to give all she has. By highlighting her gift, Jesus guides us in the way we should give: giving all we can as he gave his all for us.

Their community grows stronger day by day, drawing each of them into a deeper understanding of what it is to be loved by God and to show love in return.

Real lives

Though many think of 'The widow's mite' as a story or parable, this widow was a real person in a hard and difficult world. But it was a world where the Kingdom of God had entered, and that generosity has continued to this day in the lives of others.

The stories you are about to read here in *Simply Generous* also belong to real people living out Kingdom values in hard and difficult places. Each of them represents a prism of the light, God's generous light. They are as real as the Macedonian churches, the widow, and as you and me. They are as real as Jesus. And as real as his church.

Remember the early church? Generosity was at the very core of the first Christian community:

'They devoted themselves to the apostles' teaching and to fellowship, to the breaking of bread and to prayer. Everyone was filled with awe at the many wonders and signs performed by the apostles. All the believers were together and had everything in common. They sold property and possessions to give to anyone who had need. Every day they continued to meet together in the temple courts. They broke bread in their homes and ate together with glad and sincere hearts, praising God and enjoying the favour of all the people. And the Lord added to their number daily those who were being saved.'
(Acts 2:42–47)

Luke's description swings back and forth between outlining the way these first Christians embrace generosity and reminding us how they devote themselves to prayer, study and preaching. It's an important connection, and Luke is careful not to separate how they give from how they live as Christians.

It's a beautiful type of synergy, as the more they trust God, the freer they become with the resources at their disposal. Their community grows stronger day by day, drawing each of them into a deeper understanding of what it is to be loved by God and to show love in return.

Writing years after Jesus' death and resurrection, John – 'the disciple whom Jesus loved' – made the link clear:

'We love because he first loved us.'
(1 John 4:19)

You see, abundant love all starts at the cross, at Jesus' feet. Nowhere is it clearer than in the image of Christ on the cross, arms open wide, his invitation extended to all. As Paul writes in 2 Corinthians 8:9, 'For you know the grace of our Lord Jesus Christ, that though he was rich, yet for your sake he became poor, so that you through his poverty might become rich.'

He is a generous God in love with an impoverished people; so he gave. The disciples of Acts 2 knew this, so generosity sat at the heart of all they did. So integrated was their view of what it meant to be a Christian that there were no needy people among them. They were willing to pay, whatever the cost – financial, social, professional. Why? Because they had seen it in action in the life of Jesus himself.

Generosity today

The generous community seen in Acts is not confined to first-century history. There are plenty of examples around today – stories of God working abundantly in the lives of those who choose to express his generosity – which is why you are holding this book in your hands. We want to show what living, breathing generosity looks like and so have gathered together stories from a range of people we're inspired by.

Their backgrounds and journeys may be very different but what they all share is an understanding that answering the call to embrace generosity has sent them on some of the most fantastic, fulfilling adventures of their lives.

Of course, like the rich man in Matthew 19, the choice was theirs. Sometimes that choice will seem a little daunting, and for those committed to becoming increasingly generous there will be moments of risk ahead.

Generosity challenges so many of our assumptions about status, wealth, individual rights and personal boundaries.

'We love because he first loved us.'
(1 John 4:19)

We can be generous because he was first generous to and for us. It is that simple.

GENEROSITY'S **FIRST STEPS**

At some point in his late twenties – after a decade of living a typically hedonistic New York City adventure – Scott Harrison experienced what he calls a 'moment of introspection'. 'I was dating a model, owned a Rolex watch, a BMW, a grand piano and a golden retriever. I had ticked the boxes of success... and there was a hole, an emptiness.'

In the midst of a successful career as a nightclub promoter, Scott's moment of clarity offered a glimpse into the future. 'I saw that I would never find happiness, purpose or fulfilment in the things that I was chasing. There would never be enough girls, never be enough money, never be enough fame or status.'

Instinctively he reached back to the faith he'd turned away from at the end of his teenage years, picking up a copy of A.W. Tozer's book, *The Pursuit of God*. 'Imagine being headed in one direction and reading an inspired book from a man who is heading in the exact opposite direction – not 179 degrees or 181 but 180 degrees – the exact opposite from where I was going.'

Soon Scott was able to see his life clearly enough to be able to take his first steps back towards God. 'I hadn't lost my faith, I'd just lost obedience. I'd disobeyed for ten years, not turned into an atheist.'

Scott's initial step back towards his faith was dramatic and sudden, but it took longer for him to begin to discover more about the rest of the journey ahead of him.

'I found myself devouring the Bible, tearing through sermons, trying to find a church. I'd traded faith for something far messier – life Scott's way – for ten years. I really wanted to be authentic, but everything I was doing back in NYC was in conflict with what I was reading. So I kind of floundered.'

While there are plenty of believers who receive their calling and commission in dramatic ways, many of us experience a slower, more gradual revelation of Jesus. Our experience can be closer to that of the disciples on the road to Emmaus than to Saul's on the way to Damascus.

And so it was with Scott.

Clarity, calling and a sense of the specific adventure that God was leading him towards finally came when he left the chaos of the city and headed north to a lakeside retreat. 'I told God I would give him one year to serve him and serve the poor and see where that led.'

Scott soon found that former nightclub promoters who have yet to abandon all of their past vices are not at the top of most humanitarian organisations' recruiter lists. Every agency he applied to turned him down. He found himself caught between a desire for radical change and the reality of rejection.

Yet there was one agency that was prepared to take a risk on him. Within weeks Scott was aboard a hospital ship off the coast of Liberia, West Africa.

'Everything changed when I walked up the gangway of that ship – I gave up smoking, drinking, pornography, drugs, gambling – everything changed permanently by the grace of God.'

> I thought about how true religion is looking after the widow and orphan. Since then giving has become my joy, my freedom. Instead of holding tight, clenching my fists, I want to be open-handed.

Scott's initial year with Mercy Ships extended to two, and by the end he had seen enough poverty, enough compassion and enough of God at work to know that it was time to return to New York and encourage others to embrace generosity themselves.

'I was the most unlikely person to start a charity: a former nightclub promoter going to bring clean water to 663 million people in the world. Nightclub promoters have no concept of saving money and I was $30,000 in personal debt. Faith was so important.'

It remains equally important today. **charity: water** – the project Scott launched on his return from Africa – has grown phenomenally. In 2015 (its ninth year of operation) it raised over $35 million. But the real story is told through something better than columns on a spreadsheet, and even beyond the unique brand Scott has begun to build – a brand that makes it easy for supporters to take their own first steps in their journey of generosity.

'We've found that if we can inspire others to catch the vision they can take personal ownership. We just give them very simple tools so that they can be effective in fundraising – they're the ones that do it... and that's the secret to our fundraising success – outsourcing it to our supporters, empowering and rewarding them as they and their entire community can see what they have done.'

Ask him about defining moments and he recalls the time he accompanied a patient when they were welcomed back by their family after they had been given up for dead. 'That walk back was a turning point. I thought about how true religion is looking after the widow and orphan. Since then giving has become my joy, my freedom. Instead of holding tight, clenching my fists, I want to be open-handed.'

The solution to a life out of balance

'Save me, O God,' cries the Psalmist, 'for the waters have come up to my neck. I sink in the miry depths, where there is no foothold. I have come into the deep waters; the floods engulf me.'
(Psalm 69:1–2)

Scott Harrison was drowning in money and excess. He was in deep waters, but no depths are too great for God's rescue. And no rescue occurs without a reason.

The revelation that Scott had is not reserved for the most extreme of the prodigals or for those who travel to remote enough corners of the planet. Every one of us is in line for revelation of what it means to be a generous Christian, regardless of our location or background. All we need to do is take the first step towards it.

'Let me shout God's name with a praising song,
Let me tell his greatness in a prayer of thanks…
The poor in spirit see and are glad –
Oh, you God-seekers, take heart!
For God listens to the poor,
He doesn't walk out on the wretched.'
(Psalm 69:30, 32–33, The Message)

Far from walking out on the wretched, God offers us a part to play in his plans. We deserve none of this divine mercy, but when we accept it we instantly become recipients of God's remarkable generosity. And for so many people, this can be the first domino to fall.

> God rarely reveals the final destination of our work here on earth, but instead illumines the next step for us to take.

Perhaps from the outside it appeared implausible that a nightclub promoter would decide to volunteer for Christian mission. But to anyone who has seen their own life turned around by God, Scott's change was just another example of the power of God's grace in action. Once Scott allowed himself to be led back to God, it was entirely logical that he would allow himself to be led into a whole new adventure with God – especially one where he was given an opportunity to serve others. After all, receiving and giving are always intertwined when God's involved. It's all part of the paradoxical nature of generosity that goes to make it so infectious.

As Scott emerged from a life of hedonism, introspection and self-service, his offer to serve God and the poor for one year was just the beginning of a dramatic and radical journey that led to so much more; plenty more than he could have imagined at the time.

The same can be said for each of us: God rarely reveals the final destination of our work here on earth, but instead illumines the next step for us to take. Even though we might take it in confusion, with mixed motives and more questions than answers, we can trust God entirely.

It's so easy for us to allow life to get out of balance, to wander off course – and not just in the way that Scott did. Sure, some of us can get sidetracked by porn, drugs and hedonism, but there are other traps out there as well, and some of them are far more subtle and socially acceptable. Holidays, gifts, meals out, cars can all become traps. So can fitness, sport and online interactions; they can all so easily assume an over-inflated degree of priority in our lives. But God remains a kind and loving Father who longs to get us back on track and to weave us into his plans.

Every single one of us is a target for God's generosity. Every single one of us can receive the mercy that flows through the life, death and resurrection of Jesus. And every single one of us has the potential to see life transformed as we allow that mercy to lead us on into the adventures that God has ahead.

All that is asked of us is that we take one small step.

Ask yourself…

- What's your first memory of someone showing you generosity?
- And what's your earliest recollection of a time when you tried to be generous to someone else?
- What lessons – good and bad – did these experiences teach you about generosity?
- Scott found that being generous helped him to recalibrate his life's priorities. Is there any part of your life that you would like to see transformed?

GENEROSITY CAN BE **RISKY**

(THANK GOD)

Ansai's kidneys had failed. Both of them. With a life expectancy of five to ten years, she knew her clock was ticking.

It is a cruel irony that with time running out, Ansai had little choice other than to wait. Waiting for the next dialysis to come around. Waiting for a possible matching donor. Waiting for the day when her energy levels took yet another nosedive. Waiting became her life, and life was exhausting.

God, meanwhile, had other plans. While Ansai waited, God was stirring compassion in one of his followers. So when Pastor Tony Morley heard about the pressing need facing a member of his congregation, he and his wife Joyce prayed.

Sixty years young and in good health, with no bad habits and exercising regularly, he asked himself a simple question: why not me?

'We saw the impact of Ansai's dialysis and were moved,' he says. 'I never knew what having dialysis three times a week did to someone; how it made them weaker and weaker. So we decided I would get tested.'

The process of determining whether he could be a possible match took months; time in which to reflect on the journey he had embarked upon.

'John 13 tells us to "Love one another. In the same way I loved you, you love one another. This is how everyone will recognize that you are my disciples – when they see the love you have for each other."

'Love is incredibly practical. Joyce and I discussed this. She is a nurse so we had an idea of what we were getting into, and we talked about the risk with major surgery as well as the practical recovery issues. Everything has a cost, but love is really, really practical.'

Despite an almost 90 per cent likelihood that he wouldn't be a match, the results came back positive. He was a match. Tony was given the all-clear for surgery.

The risks of surgery failed to materialise in the operating theatre, but Tony's recovery was far from perfect. 'I was given morphine after surgery and had massive headaches. I was in hospital for six days and instead of taking six weeks my recovery took twelve.'

During those weeks Tony's family supported him and his assistant pastor cut back his paid work and devoted more time to the church. 'He was a steward,' Tony says. 'He gave time and love.'

Tony also found himself reflecting on his past. 'My father left us early in our life. My mum got kidney disease and died when I was nine. I grew up an orphan. Later, after I decided to donate, I found out Ansai's father died of the same congenital kidney disease when she was three years old. We were connected by similar pasts.'

As time passed and the risks associated with organ donation faded entirely, Tony returned to full health and gained a clear perspective on the whole episode. 'I knew I had to do something. God has been so generous to all of us, and when we look at his generosity as shown through his gift of eternal life through Jesus his son, how could I not give a possibly life saving gift? I have not a moment of regret. Every time I see Ansai now I get so much joy.'

Both Ansai and Tony continue to serve at their church, he as the Pastor and she as a member of the worship team. Together – along with the support of the wider church – they're a beautiful demonstration of what it means to be a church family. They are courageous and secure enough in their faith and relationships as a church community to be willing to embrace a significant and varied set of risks. They live and love boldly, just as Jesus taught.

For Ansai, the whole experience has taught her a profound spiritual lesson. 'I feel blessed by God's provision and deeply grateful that Pastor Tony gave me his kidney. True generosity costs. Christ sacrificed his life so we can be saved and Pastor sacrificed his kidney so I can be spared dialysis. That is true generosity. His gift has allowed me to live a normal life without the day-to-day struggles of being a dialysis patient. I am blessed.'

> God has been so generous to all of us, and when we look at his generosity as shown through his gift of eternal life through Jesus his son, how could I not give a possibly life saving gift?

Risks and rewards

'Love one another,' said Jesus. 'In the same way I loved you, you love one another.' The brand of love that Jesus demonstrated was the kind that risked everything, and its rewards were truly life changing.

Ansai's kidneys had failed, but in God's view the prognosis was not dire or even desperate. Anything but. Instead, it was an opportunity for Ansai, Pastor Tony and Joyce to say 'yes' to God's invitation. When they did, they were reminded how, in God's Kingdom, the things which we might fear will kill us sometimes end up leading us into a richer, bolder, stronger phase of life.

We might like to think otherwise, but generosity is both risky and dangerous.

We are often taught to regard risk as a negative. We are told to avoid it, or at the very least, assess it. Yet generosity offers us a different perspective, one where the risks associated are not quite the dominant force we might otherwise assume. With God, the risk is never the last word.

If there is a negative risk out there, it is the risk of choosing never to live sacrificially. If we only ever give what doesn't cost, we hold on to things in life that ultimately control us. If we allow our desires for safety and security, for love and affirmation, for wealth and status, to influence our choices, we end up isolated, weak and weary.

> Generosity offers us a different perspective, one where the risks associated are not quite the dominant force we might otherwise assume.

When we follow Jesus' instruction, something remarkable happens. We find fear's power weakening. The risks don't disappear, but above and beyond them is the all-powerful love of a God who knows us by name and longs to draw each of us closer and closer towards the freedom and life that he has designed for us.

Here on earth, it is hard to imagine a better reward.

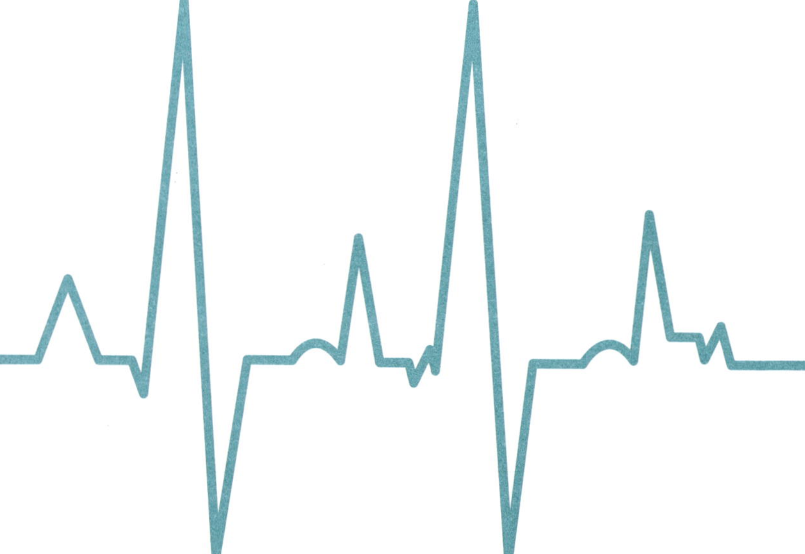

Ask yourself…

- Even though the instruction that Jesus gave us to 'love one another' is perfectly simple, we can often come up with a complex – and familiar – set of reasons for not choosing to act generously. What are the default reasons you find yourself coming up with?
- Think back to a time when you were aware of a need but chose not to be generous. What were your reasons? How much of a role did fear play in your decision? If you could revisit that time and offer yourself some advice, what would you say?
- Have you ever regretted being generous? Why? What did you learn from the experience that can help you in the future?

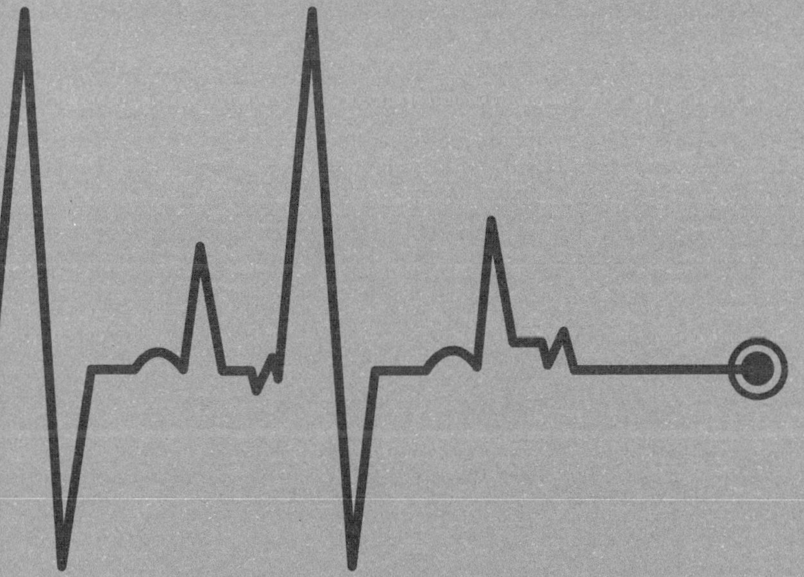

GENEROSITY **THRIVES** WHEN **PLANNED**

For Ben and Heather Grizzle, getting married didn't just mean making vows in front of their wedding guests. They made a further commitment, one that didn't make it into the ceremony, but which set their marriage on an important course. They chose to be generous in a specific, deliberate way; by increasing their giving percentage every year of their marriage.

Both Ben and Heather were encouraged to be generous from an early age. 'My parents made us tithe and then split what was left three ways between long-term savings (university), short-term savings (toys), and spending,' says Heather. 'Ben's parents shared their full budget with the kids from a young age, so they saw the real choices they were making.'

Those early experiences had a clear influence on Ben and Heather's approach to financial giving. 'We start the year, look at what our salaries will be and calculate a higher percentage for our giving than the year before,' says Heather. 'We then arrange to have that amount deducted through payroll giving, so it's in our Stewardship Giving Account and can be used when the ministries we support need it most.'

The couple's decision to weave generosity into their marriage made planned giving a key part of their approach to generosity. 'I think planning is important because it makes sure you will do it, and if you plan properly it doesn't "hurt" in quite the same way as having to write the cheque out at the end of each month. Being able to give is such an opportunity to be a part of what God is doing; it's exciting, dynamic and joy-producing. You rarely exceed goals you don't set. So you aim to give at a certain level and trust God to give you the means to reach it.'

Choosing to plan their giving has been a decision that has unleashed so much that is good in their marriage, particularly when it comes to their own faith in God. 'We have seen God do many miracles involving money throughout our marriage. God seems to particularly work through money, perhaps because it's so tangible. When he does a miracle involving money, there's no way the enemy can convince you it was just a coincidence – it is so clearly God's hand!'

> Ultimately our objective is to give all – 100% not just of our financial resources, but our hearts and passion – to Jesus.

Yet while planned giving remains vital to their expression of generosity, Ben and Heather are realists. When Ben's firm asked him to relocate to the New York office and they set about rebuilding a life with four children in tow, for the first time ever they failed to reach their giving goal.

'It was important to give ourselves grace,' says Ben. 'Sometimes the plan doesn't fully work. Though we may fall short God is still on his throne. He is still Lord and loves us.'

Seeing God at work in that way has left Ben and Heather with a clear sense of where they're heading. 'We recognise that ultimately our objective is to give all – 100% not just of our financial resources, but our hearts and passion – to Jesus, and this is one way we try to make our budget move incrementally towards that goal.'

Ben and Heather have chosen to deliberately encourage generosity among their four young children, in the way they both pray and play together as a family. They do something that Heather's parents started – giving them a fixed amount of Monopoly money to spend on movie night treats has helped their children begin to understand that stewarding our resources requires choices.

And when Abby, their eight-year-old, set up a lemonade stand outside their home they encouraged her to give away half the profits to **charity: water**. 'She wasn't sure at first, but the tips started rolling in and she made $56 in 45 minutes.

'Abby wants to stop and help every homeless person she meets in the street. One day she saw a homeless man and as we walked by tugged my hand and asked me, "Mummy can we sell my scooter so we can give this man something to eat?" I love her spirit; she would sell everything to help someone in need. I want her to be careful but I don't want to quench her spirit or plant the seed of cynicism in her.'

The search for balance between compassion and responsibility only deepens their conviction that Jesus was the ultimate giver. 'Nothing we can do can come close to the generosity he showed on the cross,' says Ben. 'How can we not go and do likewise? We firmly believe that God invites us to be co-labourers with him in building the Kingdom of God. When we give, we have an opportunity to be a part of what God is doing. Why wouldn't we want to invest?'

Planning makes perfect...

Building generosity into the routine of our lives is vital, and Peter knew it when he first wrote to the scattered believers.

'For to this you have been called, because Christ also suffered for you, leaving you an example, so that you should follow in his steps.'
(1 Peter 2:21, NRSV)

Generosity is no different. Of course there are times when we need to be open to those out-of-the-blue opportunities to demonstrate our love, gratitude and appreciation. But generosity, like all relationships, takes work, time and consistent effort. We can't just dip our hand in our pocket when we feel sufficiently moved. If we are to fulfil our potential and discover the full impact that God can have on our lives, we have to make time and space to allow generosity to thrive.

And we need to take the time to sow the seed and nurture the habit in the next generation.

The phrase 'so that you might follow in his steps' is only used once in the New Testament. It comes from a Greek root word that suggests a student tracing every letter of his teacher exactly. We have been called to follow Jesus more closely than we might imagine.

Following in God's steps means making a deliberate choice to demonstrate our love for God and others. It means making a priority of being generous, and recognising that there will always be more to discover.

It means making a priority of being generous, and recognising that there will always be more to discover.

How we choose to be generous with the resources at our disposal will be unique to every one of us, but by planning to give away more and more with each passing year, we set up ourselves – and those we share our lives with – for a wonderful adventure with God.

Ask yourself…

- What has God given to you in terms of time, talent and resources? Make a list of what you are a steward over. Why did the Lord give you these unique resources and not someone else? What are the things only you can do with and for him?
- When were you last spontaneous in your giving? Do you deliberately put yourself in situations where you might sense the opportunity to give, or do you tend to avoid them?
- When did you last examine your giving? What plans can you put in place to be more generous in the future? What do you see as the advantages and disadvantages of spontaneous giving over planned giving?
- How can you build generosity into your relationships more effectively?

GENEROSITY **COSTS,** BUT IT ALSO **TRANSFORMS**

Rich Stanton's life is a tale of extremes. His teenage years were a collision of illness, bad choices and relentless pain that threatened to cut his life short. But they are not the only acute forces at play. There is grace and there is love. And there are two truly remarkable acts of generosity that have transformed everything about him.

Growing up in a deprived corner of South Wales, Rich knew that life could be tough. 'I found it hard to fit in,' he says. 'When I was 14, I was taken out of mainstream education and put into a child psychiatric unit.'

As a young child his relationship with his parents had been fine, but as troubles stacked up in his teenage years, life at home had deteriorated. 'I started to resent them, and when my dad became a Christian when I was 14 he had a peace and tranquility about him that I hated.'

So when he was thrown out of the child psychiatric unit for his unmanageable behaviour, Rich's return home was never going to be easy. He tried to stab his father at one point, and then, a month or so later, got drunk and turned the knife on himself for an hour. It took a squad car full of policemen to get him to stop and almost 40 stitches in hospital to close the wounds.

The next four years were a blur of drug abuse, petty crime and dangerous companions. When Rich and a friend ran out of drugs during a party one night, the two of them robbed and assaulted a local dealer. Arrested the next day, Rich knew that he was looking at four years for aggravated burglary. 'I knew I couldn't stand being locked up again, and I planned to take my own life if I was convicted. So I lied to the police, trying to get myself out of trouble.' When they accepted his version of events, dropped the charge to common assault and gave him a £100 fine, Rich was shocked.

Rich noticed within him a new desire to turn his life around. Splitting up with his girlfriend – a heroin addict – was the logical first step to make, but how to fully get his life back on track? How could he ever hope to fully recover from so desperate a place?

The answer came from his parents, the very people he had threatened and assaulted, those whose lives he had dogged with pain and worry. 'I phoned my mum and told her that I didn't know what was happening to me or what I should do. She said, "Why don't you move back home?" and it hit me like a ton of bricks. I never expected her to say that.

'So I turned up at the house, holding all that I had in one little bag, and knocked on the door. As soon as it opened I could feel it; the sense of peace hit me. I took one step inside into the same tranquility that I had hated in my dad. Now I was experiencing it for myself.'

Rich started attending church, and it was not long before he sensed that God was presenting him with an invitation; if Rich followed Jesus then everything would be forgiven and his life would have purpose.

'When I used to self-harm I felt as though tension and anger flowed out of me along with the blood. But sitting at the back of the church I felt forgiveness wash over me.' God was offering him the chance of something he never thought he could have: a fresh start.

And so it began, the rebuild of Rich's life. His sense of freedom and forgiveness was tangible, and some transformations were instant – like an end to the self-harming. 'The hard work of discipleship took longer, and it was one year before I was free from drugs and another 12 months before I had conquered the binge drinking. It took even longer to deal with the anger and hurt that had been inside me for so long.'

Early on in his new life as a Christian, Rich knew that he wanted to become the kind of mentor to other young people that he didn't have when he was younger. He became a youth worker, enrolled in Bible college and eventually took a job working with Manchester's Message Trust, helping oversee the Eden project. Eden teams move into some of the country's toughest estates, places just like the community in which Rich grew up. Rich's experiences lead him into some remarkable conversations, and for many of the young people he talks with it is only when they see his scars that they finally believe that such a gentle, encouraging man could have so turbulent a past. In those moments, his scars are more than a sign of damage; they're a powerful symbol of Jesus' rescue.

Rich often talks about the fact that the moment when his parents invited him home was the first of two pivotal moments that changed his life. It was the perfect demonstration of their grace, their generosity and their love, and it laid the foundations for God's own offer to Rich. Having seen the impact of faith on the life of his father, Rich was better able to hear and respond to the call of his heavenly Father as well.

And there was yet another ripple that was started by that initial act of generosity. Rich has chosen to work with Eden because he believes that God works best through us when we decide to give and not count the cost. Like so many others in this book, Rich knows that generosity is costly, but the cost of giving is always less than the reward.

Rich knows that generosity is costly, but the cost of giving is always less than the reward.

'My faith,' says Rich, 'has been shaken in various ways. But it will never fail because of that one experience of God giving me forgiveness.'

When grace and generosity collide

God's gift was enough to break the deadlock within Rich. It was the perfect solution, just as it was in the parable of the prodigal son. Rich knows that, like the father Jesus described in his story, his own parents had good reason to let their son face the consequences of his actions alone, and good reason to fear what might happen if he came back. Instead they chose to offer open arms and graceful acceptance, to risk giving their son another chance.

'Quick.'

In Jesus' parable, it's the first word that the wayward, starving, prodigal son hears from his loving father. The young man has arrived with a speech ready to deliver, one that acknowledges his sins – against God and against his own father – and declares that he is no longer fit to be called his son.

But his father cuts him off before he can finish.

'"Quick," he says. "Bring a clean set of clothes and dress him. Put the family ring on his finger and sandals on his feet. Then get a grain-fed heifer and roast it. We're going to feast! We're going to have a wonderful time! My son is here – given up for dead and now alive! Given up for lost and now found!" And they began to have a wonderful time.'
(Luke 15:22–24, The Message)

'Quick' perfectly encapsulates the heart behind the words and actions of Rich's parents when they took him into their forgiving arms. They did not hold generosity back or choose to defer it until such a time as they deemed wise. Generosity was not a reward for a sustained period of good behaviour. It was an expression of love, grace and the power of God to heal even the deepest wounds.

Of course there are times when generosity requires careful thought, sustained commitment and wise counsel. But every once in a while there are days when generosity calls for our urgent response, no matter what the risks, no matter what the cost.

Inspired by grace, led by the Spirit, those are the days when we risk everything. Those are the days when lives can be transformed in an instant.

> Generosity was not a reward for a sustained period of good behaviour. It was an expression of love, grace and the power of God to heal even the deepest wounds.

Ask yourself...

- Have you ever been on the receiving end of the kind of grace that Rich received? Do you remember what it felt like at the time? How did it change the way you thought about both yourself and God?
- What's the biggest, most generous risk you've ever taken? How did it work out for you and the recipient? What would you do differently if faced with the same situation again?
- Are there situations where you feel weary from trying hard but seeing no change? Could there be room for a little more grace-inspired generosity?

GENEROSITY IS INFECTIOUS

This little acorn began six years ago, to turn Lent upside down, on its head, and instead of giving up, the idea was to give out with a simple generous act for 40 days. And so 40acts was created.

No one at Stewardship would have predicted that within six years over 100,000 folk would sign up and embrace Lent so differently. The acorn was planted, put down firm roots, opened up and unleashed a wave of national generosity.

Purple-clad bishops at Leicester railway station gave out sweet treats to amused commuters; schoolchildren from Exeter to Dumfries paid each other compliments. Gardens were weeded, chocolate distributed, new friendships created, old friendships renewed, presents delivered, skills shared, barriers removed, love exchanged and reconciliations made.

'40acts is a fantastic excuse to go and do something slightly out of the ordinary, to step out of my comfort zone and to start a conversation,' observed one keen supporter.

Forty days of generous acts have become an antidote to our self-absorbed lives with our 'to-do lists', agendas and me-first attitude.

When Debbie Wright began working for Stewardship, Lent was approaching and she heard the familiar conversations among her friends about whether to give up coffee or chocolate, TV or Facebook, and it struck her again how odd it all was. Yes, she thought, sacrifice and discipline are all well and good, but somehow Lent seemed to have more to do with health kicks than spiritual preparation. It all felt a little too inward-looking and about myself.

A fortnight into her new job at Stewardship, and her decision to take the post seemed in some way related to her Lent musings. 'I didn't want to be in a job where generosity was solely about how much money you could give. Fortunately for me, Stewardship wanted to talk about generosity in a broad and holistic way, focusing on being generous with your time, talents, skills and attitude as well as money. That's what convinced me to take the job.'

Debbie's thoughts about Lent burned deep enough within her to make her consider sharing them with her boss, Daniel Jones. He'd been wrestling too, wondering how to get good teaching on generosity into churches. Having tried to reach church leaders, he was steering Stewardship towards a different route: trying to reach the people in the pews directly.

'I didn't know Daniel very well at the time,' says Debbie, 'but I floated the idea and suggested publishing 40 reflections as a challenge over Lent. Without a minute's hesitation, he said yes!' Other team members bought into the vision and between them they came up with a list of 40 people to write the reflections – about a quarter being staff and the rest church, work or family connections.

And so 40acts was born. The plan was simple: to send to subscribers a Bible-based reflection on a particular aspect of generosity twinned with a practical challenge to benefit others. That first year was a hand-to-mouth affair, with only half the contributions written by the time Lent began, but there were already signs that pairing Lent with generosity was a compelling proposition.

Mike O'Neill, Stewardship's Chief Executive, knew that if the campaign were to spread, it would need support, and others quickly came on board. 'That whole first year made me realise that the essence of 40acts is relationships. In giving out, you open up someone's ability to receive and in that process a conversation starts.'

'Generosity is incredibly infectious and every year we are taken aback,' reflects Daniel. 'Just before Lent begins, I always wonder whether we have done the right thing or whether everyone will have moved on to something else, but then the number of subscribers jumps up and up. We have never had any formal marketing or advertising; people just share the idea, email to email, text to text, and by Twitter retweets and good old word of mouth. There is just something incredibly compelling and attractive about living a life that puts generosity first, puts others first.'

About 1500 people signed up to give out rather than give up with 40acts in 2011. In 2012 that number jumped to 5000. By the time 2016 came around, subscriber numbers exceeded 103,000. By giving permission to break free from our reserved culture, 40acts has helped people speak to strangers, forge deeper relationship with their neighbours and take risks that they might otherwise have stepped back from.

Over the years the campaign has received awards and accolades, but the real trophies are the stories that come from participants themselves. Like the time in 2014 when two 40act-ers independently started giving out chocolate to strangers on the same crowded commuter train for Chocolate Tuesday, sparking a surge of Twitter interest and appreciation.

Then there was the Muslim man in the fourth year who wrote to say that signing up to 40acts had played a key role in helping him learn to admire the Christian faith and become more tolerant. And the girl in her 20s in Northern Ireland who came back to faith as 40acts created something that was relevant, community-based and focused on others.

> We receive so that we can give, and give because we have received.

Over the years 40acts has partnered with a number of different organisations, but the connections have been more than strategic or tactical. Instead, 40acts has grown because individuals have caught the vision for themselves.

For Sam Donoghue of *Childrenswork* magazine, this new view of Lent made perfect sense: 'I'd done the giving-up bit and was more than ready to take on something new. I loved the kids' resources in the campaign – kids really get generosity and the graciousness of God.'

I have become much more aware of trying to be a generous person and more aware of other people.

Despite 40acts growing bigger with each year, the original team remains in place. More significantly, they can testify to the enduring, infectious benefits of embracing generosity in this way.

'I have become much more aware of trying to be a generous person and more aware of other people,' says Debbie. 'In everything – chance encounters, family, church life, friends – I find now that I have a slightly different mindset. I find it terribly sad that we live in such a self-centred world. Look at the Lord's Prayer. It's OUR Father, not my Father. I see 40acts as a way to get community back for everyone. It's certainly touched me and made me think anew.'

40acts helps turn observers into givers, and strangers into receivers. It is as accessible as it is infectious, and is only just beginning.

The joy of God's economy

'He throws caution to the winds,
giving to the needy in reckless abandon.
His right-living, right-giving ways
never run out, never wear out.'
(2 Corinthians 9:9, The Message)

There's something wonderful about these words, especially if you're 'the needy' – the kind of people who were such clear beneficiaries of the generosity of the early church (see Acts 2:44–45). But what about those that aren't? What about if you're the kind of person who knows far less about being *in need* than they do about being *in want*?

Seen through God's eyes, what do our lives of plenty and abundance look like?

Paul also says to the church in Corinth: 'God can pour on the blessings in astonishing ways so that you're ready for anything and everything, more than just ready to do what needs to be done' (v. 8).

You have money? That's good. You've got enough food and shelter to be able to consider giving up a certain treat or a social activity throughout Lent? That's good too.

In fact it's a clear reason for rejoicing, for 'He gives you something you can then give away, which grows into full-formed lives, robust in God, wealthy in every way, so that you can be generous in every way, producing with us great praise to God' (v. 11).

The economy of God doesn't work the same way that our lives may do. Financial wealth can sometimes drive us away from each other; to live in bigger houses, to move into nicer neighbourhoods, to eat in better restaurants and to take nicer holidays – all of which bring us into contact with a narrower range of people. Living this way, eventually we mix only with those who are like us.

God does things differently. Look at the early church, where a diverse range of believers shared what they had. Persecuted and under threat, they did not retreat or close themselves off. Instead they chose to live in true generosity and grew exponentially.

We receive so that we can give, and give because we have received. And at every stage of the adventure we find ourselves tethered to God himself, and invited to join in his work with him as he propels us out to do the work of his Kingdom among the people he created. The rich and the poor, the socially desirable and the hard to love. God invites us to look upon them all the way he does, with generous love.

40acts isn't the only campaign that helps propel people out to be generous, and it's not the best one either. But if 40acts has achieved anything that could be considered a success, it is thanks only to the infectious nature of God's generosity, and the courage and enthusiasm of everyday Christians who have decided to take a risk and say 'yes' to God.

Whether we're receiving or giving, our role is essentially the same: to say 'yes' God, to choose to love him, to not hold on to blessings or gifts or live in fear or insecurity.

The result is the same too: lives fully formed, dependent on God, open to being used by him.

Ask yourself...

- The 40acts story is all about infectious generosity, but it is only ever made up of individual moments where people decide to take a chance and act generously. Does that sound too much for you? Are you left thinking, 'I could never do that'? Consider praying for God's overflow into your life, asking him to prove you wrong.
- What would it look like for you to embrace infectious generosity next time Lent comes around (or even before)? What are the current boundaries that you've put in place around what you give or how you guard your privacy?
- What area of your life do you think God wants you to give more in? Why? What is your plan to increase your giving?

GENEROSITY BUILDS CHARACTER

For Tony Woodward, the journey of generosity started more than 70 years ago. At the family dining table he listened to his parents as they talked about the missionaries they supported in far-flung places.

'This was long before the internet and email,' Tony says. 'We would parcel up goods or send money and then not hear anything, often for months. Then out of the blue one of those flimsy airmail letters would arrive, usually recounting God's wonderful timing. I remember one family were about to sell all their wedding presents for much-needed food when our gift arrived. These events had a profound effect on me which I have carried through my life.'

It was a profound effect that lasted way beyond childhood. When he started his first job in the 1960s, shortly after graduating from university, Tony chose to keep a written record of his monthly giving.

'I called it the Lord's Portion,' he says. 'In the first month I gave £11 away: £5 to our church, £3 to a local Christian worker and £3 to a mission agency. From then on, every month's giving has been duly recorded.'

Tony and his wife Sylvia's lifetime of giving has been mapped out in a series of ledgers. The beautiful script doesn't just tell the story of the changes in Christian social action over the decades; it also reveals the way in which the couple have allowed their compassion to be directed by God. The care with which they have recorded their giving reflects the value they place on generosity; it has always been a significant part of their lives, a subject of much prayer, discussion and joy.

Tony and Sylvia Woodward wouldn't identify themselves as particularly generous, yet the planning and recording of their giving has remained a constant feature of their marriage, and one that continues today.

Occasionally they have had to adjust their giving in response to other factors. 'There have been times in our lives when exceptional circumstances have meant we had to cut back in some way,' says Tony. 'But,' adds Sylvia, 'we have always tried to make up the gap later on, so our giving has remained constant.'

Free from a legalistic approach to giving, Tony and Sylvia's decades-long journey of generosity has deepened their love for God, as Tony explains: '1 Corinthians 16:1–4 reminds us that Christians should give regularly and systematically. It doesn't matter how much; tithing is a practice of the Old Testament whereas the New Testament teaches that we ought to give joyfully and also have some over to give spontaneously. To us, giving is an expression of appreciation for what the Lord has done for us.'

Generosity is also a tool that God appears to use to regularly encourage Tony and Sylvia. Some time ago they decided to send care gifts to missionaries they support abroad. One such family was doing medical work in Pakistan. Their area suddenly became dangerous and they were ordered by the Pakistani Government to leave immediately. The care package had arrived exactly the day before but they hadn't opened it. Just before they began their two-day journey to the airport, they opened the

> As Billy Graham once said, "God has given us two hands – one to receive with and the other to give with. We are not cisterns made for hoarding; we are channels made for sharing."

box. The food we sent blessed them on their journey. When they reached safety, they wrote thanking Tony and Sylvia for prayerfully thinking of them.

The ledgers reveal not just how the world has changed since Tony first heard stories of missionaries serving the Lord in remote locations but also how Tony and Sylvia themselves have changed. One of their most recent entries was made following a missionary trip to Africa. Tony had been invited to Niamey, Niger, to teach a course at a Bible school on 'The Principles of Christian Stewardship'. People there asked him not only to write a curriculum on Stewardship for them but also to teach them how to give. Tony is now hoping to return one day to continue teaching. Meanwhile, the course material is available for use elsewhere.

With three granddaughters finishing their university studies and embarking on their professional careers, Tony and Sylvia are aware of the pressures of modern living.

'I think it is much harder now for young people starting out in life, with an economic downturn, student loans and debt, but also the lure of materialism and a wealth of choice that just didn't exist 50 years ago. Our advice to our granddaughters is to avoid frivolous debt at all costs, put God first and always give with a glad heart.

'As Billy Graham once said, "God has given us two hands – one to receive with and the other to give with. We are not cisterns made for hoarding; we are channels made for sharing."'

The two hands of generosity

Turn the clock back and it is possible to see a foreshadowing of Tony and Sylvia's embrace of planned giving in scripture.

1 Chronicles 29 recalls how King David urged all the people of Israel to contribute to the building of the temple in Jerusalem. He chose to model the type of generosity he envisaged by giving 'over and above' (v. 3) from his personal wealth. The people followed suit and experienced a similar degree of joy and freedom as a result.

Closing in prayer, King David exemplifies the generosity-shaped character:

'But who am I? And who are my people? Without your help we wouldn't be able to give this much. Everything comes from you. We've given back to you only what comes from you.'
(1 Chronicles 29:14, NIRV)

Tony's first lessons took place as he sat and listened to his parents talking, but his God-scripted education continued way beyond that, long into adulthood. As the years passed and his giving continued, Tony learned to appreciate the way that generosity deepened his faith.

None of us are too old, too mean or too generous to give, to receive or to learn another lesson from God.

He may have long since left the dining table, but Tony – like King David, Billy Graham and millions more besides – has learned that none of us are too old, too mean or too generous to give, to receive or to learn another lesson from God.

So often those lessons are learned through constant repetition and practice. So while choosing to keep a record of what we give, or deciding to give cheerfully no matter what our personal circumstance, might seem small and almost insignificant, these are the kind of choices that will serve us well on our journey of generosity. After all, what is character other than the choices we make?

Ask yourself...

- Who are the people and what are the causes that you want to support throughout your lifetime? Imagine you're in Tony's position, looking back on a lifetime of generosity. What would give you happiness? Would you have any cause for regret?
- Planned giving is an important part of generosity, just as spontaneous giving (see page 22) and grace-driven generosity (see page 34) have their place. Which of these three comes most easily to you? Which one do you struggle with?
- What parts of your character have been shaped by generosity? What lessons have you learned through both giving and receiving? Are you hungry for more?
- Who else do you know who is truly generous? How has their character been shaped by their giving?

GENEROSITY
IS MESSY,

BUT IT CLEARS
THINGS UP

'Last week I gave away my TV because my neighbour needed one,' says Danielle Marshall.

If you feel as though you know where this story is going, think again. Not long after Danielle handed the set over, there was another knock on her door. It was the neighbour again. Had she returned with a token of her appreciation? Not quite.

'She said there was a missing lead and she was really cross about it. I felt so annoyed with her! But it made me think: am I really just OK to be generous when I have chosen it, or only when people are appreciative? I want to be in a better place. I am nowhere near where I want to be, and I have so much to learn.'

Danielle's life is full of stories like this, experiences that aren't black and white but that are complicated and real. We all face the temptation to construct a life that is safe, comfortable and manageable, but Danielle is the kind of person who chooses the opposite. She chooses to get messy. Giving up occasional electrical goods is just the tip of the iceberg.

Where it all began is hard to tell. Was it when her father made his children an offer of 15 pence pocket money each week with no obligation to give any away, or 20 pence with a mandatory tithe? Was it when her parents chose to live in a smaller house so that they could fund various university places for people outside their family? Or was it the point when Danielle abandoned her teenage ambitions to be a lawyer and chose a career in nursing instead?

What is clear is that when she left home Danielle faced one of her greatest choices, a decision that would go on to shape her character in ways she would never have predicted at the time. She chose to move into one of the toughest estates in her town, a place infamous for drugs and violence. 'I was living in a nice part of town, and one day I felt God say "You need to move to the estate." I told him, "No way" and put some music on.' Later, when a friend phoned with the same message, Danielle hung up.

Yet within months – thanks to the generosity of another friend who bought a flat for them to live in – Danielle and her friend were living on the estate. Over a decade later and there are plenty of stories to share: of new friends turning up after a knife fight and asking for prayer and help; of frightened neighbours asking Danielle to pray for safety and then returning wide-eyed the following week to tell her that the estate had been free from gun crime and all other violence; of the dozen other members of their church who have chosen to move onto the estate.

For every headline of triumph there is a deeper story of God at work among the mess and complexity of real life. Not long after she moved, Danielle discovered her first challenge. 'I moved here so that I could build real relationships with people – but at first it was all on my terms. When they started dropping in at other times I felt challenged about how generous I was really being. To give money is one thing, but what about the whole of me? Jesus gave it all, so what about my life? Am I available?

'I've seen God do more *in* me than *through* me, and I love watching what God is doing. He's slowly killing my pride. I don't have a career and it leaves me wondering what all this downward mobility really means. When God's given me a brain, does not using it mean I am being a bad steward? But when I remember that Jesus left heaven and became a servant, surely I can lose some of my middle-classness and serve others?'

There is another vital lesson that messy generosity has taught Danielle. Now she knows how her happiness can be suffocated. There is something toxic about the habit of 'looking around at my friends and comparing myself, thinking about where I was at school and what I could have achieved academically or career-wise'. But that is not the end of the story. 'When I focus on who Jesus has called me to love, then I am content.'

As every person who chooses to serve others soon learns, Danielle knows that generosity is not a solo sport. 'I came here thinking that we had so much to teach, so much to offer, but I now know that I have so much to learn. They have taught me how to be a good neighbour and they are much better at looking after me than I am at looking after them.

> I've seen God do more *in* me than *through* me, and I love watching what God is doing. He's slowly killing my pride.

'I can only be generous because of what God and others have given me. When I moved I felt like God said that my flat would be a haven for people and a place where people who are at sixes and sevens would come and find healing. But I started to panic as I wasn't sure that on a low salary (that didn't even cover my living expenses) I could continue feeding and watering lots of others too. Yet we've always had enough food for everyone that's come over – whether they are invited or unexpected guests! And none of this would have happened without others being obedient to God with the things they have been given. I am so grateful to him and humbled by his kindness, and the kindness of others who are also very generous.'

Messy? Yes, but for a reason…

'Whoever wants to be my disciple must deny themselves and take up their cross and follow me.' Jesus' words in Matthew 16:24 can send shivers down the spine. After all, crosses lead to crucifixion. Do all true disciples have to become martyrs?

In fact, Jesus was encouraging his disciples to think about sacrifice in a different way. Not as a single event at the end of life, but as a habit of saying 'no' to taking control of our own lives and 'yes' to spending what we have for the sake of Jesus.

It's a unique type of sacrifice, as Jesus makes clear by continuing with the promise that 'whoever loses their life for me will find it'.

Danielle's story shows this type of sacrifice in action. Like so many other Christians, she is in the habit of saying 'no' to a neat life and 'yes' to a messy one, the sort that is a blend of unexpected visitors, complicated relationships and outrageous requests. Generosity is not a one-off occurrence, nor is it a case of her giving what she can easily live without. It's not even about simply moving onto a run-down council estate in the hope of making a grand gesture. Instead, we see generosity flourish in the daily actions of a life shared with others.

Like so many other Christians, she is in the habit of saying 'no' to a neat life and 'yes' to a messy one, the sort that is a blend of unexpected visitors, complicated relationships and outrageous requests.

So many of the influences around us would teach us the opposite: to be closed, to be private, to control our lives. We are urged to compare ourselves with others, to make sure that we match up to the pack's aspirations and achievements. There's no true freedom down that path. Life may feel neater, but it's as nothing compared with the life that flows when we focus on who Jesus would have us love.

Nothing else comes close.

Ask yourself…

- What cultural barriers do you have in place that keep you from forming deeper relationships with people in need?
- With so much need around us, it can be hard to know which particular cause to take up. Do you ever feel as though you've picked up the wrong cross?
- What's the main area in which you need to learn how to be more content? How would that change how you see the rest of your life?
- God places us in situations and with people he wants us to be in relationship with. Who are the people that you know God is calling you to love?
- Sometimes our generosity puts us on the front line, but God often uses our resources to help others put God's compassion into action. The Good Samaritan handed over the wounded traveller to the innkeeper. Are you ready to use your resources to invite others in to help?

GENEROSITY WILL CHANGE YOU MORE THAN YOU THINK

For Rose, generosity was a topic she never heard all that much about when she was growing up. 'I don't think I was ever taught about giving, either at home, at school, or at church. Money just wasn't really talked about.'

By the time she left college and started working, that lack of teaching quickly started to show. 'I got into difficulty when I received an offer of a credit card through the post. I signed up without really thinking about it, and that's when the trouble started; I built up a debt. I thought I could pay it off at the end of the month but, despite making repayments, the amount just seemed to increase every month.'

The result was more than a rise in her anxiety levels and a drop in her disposable income. 'I felt ashamed and out of control. I lived at home with my parents but could never own up to the fact that I had a problem. Instead, I moved the debt from one credit card to another, trying to manage the situation entirely on my own. It was a really lonely period in my life; I didn't feel I could talk to my family, friends, or anyone at church.'

Change, however, was close at hand. Still in debt, Rose started attending a different church, took on a role as a volunteer intern and, for the first time in her life, heard biblical teaching about giving and tithing. 'My initial reaction was that I couldn't afford to give, but as I learnt more I realised that as a disciple of Christ I should take hold of my finances. I started with very small amounts and soon realised that this sacrificial giving was important to me, my faith, and my relationship with God.

'I still can't explain how it happened, but my debt disappeared. I was earning very little from a part-time job in a local supermarket and I think it was no longer "easy come, easy go", relying on the pay cheque at the end of the month. I set a budget, gave, saved, and by the end of my training I had paid off my debt.'

Ten years have passed since then and Rose continues to give regularly to her church. 'I still have a credit card today, and I still have things to learn about managing finances, but I set a budget and loosely stick to it, though I could do better. But my faith in God's provision has grown so much it's made giving much easier.

'I didn't start out giving 10 per cent but I did get to that level over time, and a few years ago I was inspired by another couple's story and decided to challenge myself, and possibly God too, to increase my giving by one per cent each year. A few weeks after making that decision, I was awarded a pay rise at work. I was completely blown away by the generosity of my employer and God's faithfulness in provision.'

But she has experienced a change to more than her spending patterns. 'I've gained more knowledge of biblical stewardship and also feel responsible for what I have been given. But the greatest change of all comes from the fact that I've seen the inexplicable generosity of God in so many different ways.'

Soon after she got married, Rose decided to leave her job for health reasons. She wondered about looking for something else to ensure that she could keep on contributing financially to the household, but her husband suggested that she gave time instead to work for the church. 'I was easily persuaded when my husband pointed out that the monetary value of my voluntary hours at church, even if you calculated them just as minimum wage, easily outweighed the value of a tithe on the salary I would have earned. It was the first time I'd really thought about the value of giving in a way other than hard cash.'

Unexpected blessings have continued to spring up, and Rose is continually reminded that it is impossible for her to out-give God.

'God has blessed me with my giving, my release from debt, and opened my eyes to the many ways of measuring generosity.'

The case against generosity

The reasons not to give may appear complicated as well as pretty numerous. But boil them down and there's often one clear, simple barrier to our embracing generosity. Fear.

When Jesus appeared to his disciples not long after his crucifixion and burial, he encountered plenty of fear. 'Peace be with you!' he said in greeting as he appeared in front of them. Peace? They needed an awful lot of it.

'But they were startled and frightened and thought they saw a spirit. And he said to them, "Why are you troubled, and why do doubts arise in your hearts? See my hands and my feet, that it is I myself. Touch me, and see. For a spirit does not have flesh and bones as you see that I have."'
(Luke 24:37–39, ESV)

It was the fear that troubled them. Seeing his hands and feet may only have intensified their anxiety – reminding them how precarious their situation was. But while Jesus could so easily have lost the scars, he chose to keep them; a reminder of the sacrifice he made, the battle he won, the gift he gave.

So many of us have echoed Rose's thoughts over the years. We struggle to see how we can get out of debt, feeling as though we are trapped by it, fearful that trouble is just around the corner. We fear letting go; we worry that if we choose to be generous we will somehow find ourselves weaker, poorer and more vulnerable.

And yet Jesus has the power to break in and change everything. He can change our fears and he can change our confusion about the fact that generosity will always leave a positive mark upon us.

In the same way that he released the disciples from fear and anxiety, he revealed to Rose the truth about generosity: that it is a path to worshipping God, a route that takes us out of our own self-made prisons and into freedom once more.

Many of us know what it is to feel a little ashamed and to not want to talk to anyone about debt. God does not deal in shame any more than he deals in fear.

Instead he comforts us, reassures us, and then shows us the way out to go and help others.

Jesus has the power to break in and change everything. He can change our fears and he can change our confusion about the fact that generosity will always leave a positive mark upon us.

Ask yourself…

- Do you think that it sounds unwise to give while you are in debt financially? If you do, what's the counter-argument? Is there a chance that giving changes you and allows God a little more control in your life?
- Time, talent, money – the three classic resources with which we can be generous. What do you feel you need to give more of?
- Rose made a plan to give more away with each passing year. If you don't do that yet, take time to think and pray about it.
- How has generosity shaped you? If that's a hard question to answer, ask yourself why it's so difficult.

GENEROSITY'S JOURNEY LEADS US TO NEW DESTINATIONS

Dr Nathalie MacDermott was barely a teenager when she knew that one day she would end up working with Ebola patients. It was little more than a hunch, but when she turned 20 and became a Christian the sense of Ebola being a God-given calling became even stronger.

Even so, there were more years to wait before the hunch turned into any kind of reality. 'For many years I felt like I was waiting for the opportunity to respond to what I believed God was calling me to do.'

Yet her journey of generosity was not at all stuck. It was simply progressing in ways she was unaware of. A couple of summers spent serving in an orphanage in Belarus taught her to trust God no matter how bleak the prospects, as well as to expect him to provide in miraculous ways.

'I would pray over the children. One of them had been born with cerebral palsy and hydrocephalus. He was eight years old but the size of a two-year-old. He could only lie on one side or the other because his spine stuck out and he had tremendous pressure sores on his hips, the skin rubbed raw and worn down to the bone. The year before we'd worked hard on these sores and left special dressings and he'd made improvements, but we had not been able to leave enough for the whole year. So when we returned the sores had got bad again.

'One day the boy vomited everywhere so I picked him up and took him outside while one of my colleagues changed his cot. I sat on the sofa in the play area and started talking to God about him. "I just don't understand why he's still here. He's in so much pain, suffering so much. Anyone who has anything to learn from this little guy must have learned it already so please will you either miraculously heal him or take him to be with you. But please don't leave him like this." I put him back in his cot and the next morning at 6am he died. What an answer to prayer; he is in heaven now, running around with legs that work. I think it would have been amazing to see the other, but I think I only had a glimmer of the faith needed for that.'

A glimmer of faith it might have been, but it was enough to lead Nathalie into some remarkable adventures. Especially when new opportunities to be generous with her faith started to present themselves.

One of the first was a summer trip to the Middle East and South-East Asia – into countries where Bibles are scarce and Christians are at risk. Nathalie and a friend delivered Bibles to underground Christians and the experience increased her appetite for taking risks for God. Later on, stints volunteering among cholera patients in Haiti and victims of cyclone Haiyan in the Philippines brought her face to face with those in desperate need of God's intervention. Time and time again, she saw God invite her to join in his work. 'It was as if God kicked the door open in front of me and shoved me through it.'

In the summer of 2014 Nathalie began the first of what would be two trips to Liberia over the coming months. Working with Samaritan's Purse she cared for the sick and dying, established protocols to stop Ebola spreading and watched as two American colleagues – Nancy Writebol and Kent Brantly – became the first westerners to contract the deadly virus.

'Liberia showed me that even if the absolute worst happens – which it did in that first trip – God is faithful and he will bring us through. He will show us the way out. As Nancy put it, "God was good before I had Ebola, he was good while I had it and he is good after it. Even if I died from Ebola he still would have been good." She never doubted it. She was never shaken.'

After a decade of taking a series of small steps in her generous adventure with God, Nathalie is clear about the core lesson she has learned: 'God is faithful. In the midst of everything, it's worth risking everything for Him.

'There have been challenges that might have shaken other people, but they've not shaken my faith. I've had doubts and questions, but I know God is sovereign. I accept that some things in life will be unknown. That's just the way it is. I've prayed for a lot of children and many of them have died while some have been miraculously healed. I can't tell you why, but I know that God is good.'

Haiti, the Philippines, Liberia – Nathalie's journey has already taken her to so many different locations and given her a front-row view of God in action among some of the poorest, most needy communities.

God was good before I had Ebola, he was good while I had it and he is good after it. Even if I died from Ebola he still would have been good.

But while the destinations are often far-flung and the environments extreme, Nathalie's faith journey has been measured in small steps rather than giant leaps. If we trust God day to day, practise saying 'yes' to the opportunities he places in front of us and give what we have without counting the cost, each of us will find ourselves moving in the right direction.

Further up and further in.

Direction not destination

Most of the time we know exactly where we're going. Whether it's booking a holiday or making a weekend road trip, when we start out we have a destination in mind. Knowing our end point allows us to plan. It helps us pace ourselves. It puts us in control.

God's journeys are different. We hardly ever know the destination and our plans so often end up in the bin. And as for being in control...

And all of this is good news, as the Psalmist makes clear:

'Your thunder was heard in the whirlwind,
your lightning lit up the world;
the earth trembled and quaked.
Your path led through the sea,
your way through the mighty waters,
though your footprints were not seen.
You led your people like a flock
by the hand of Moses and Aaron.'
(Psalm 77:18–20)

The last verse is the route planner for every generous journey. God leads with us and has us lead with each other; there is only one hand, the hand of Moses and Aaron. It's a picture of community and unity; of all hands becoming one when we move in his way, follow his path, search out his footprints.

All we have to do is take the next small step, believing in the faithful goodness of a God who performs miracles. All we have to do is walk.

There is no mention of the destination, only the direction.

All we have to do is take the next small step, believing in the faithful goodness of a God who performs miracles. All we have to do is walk.

For years Nathalie has done precisely that. It has taken her from Haiti to the Philippines, from Laos to Liberia. She has seen and been in deep waters, experienced whirlwinds and the rumbles of an earth crying out for generosity to be put into action.

Never has she travelled alone.

Ask yourself...

- Have you ever been through an experience which was lonely at the time but in which, in hindsight, you realised God was with you? What lesson was God teaching you through it?
- What would it look like for you to take a step into the unknown with God?
- If that previous one is a hard question to answer, ask yourself how you feel about not being able to answer it. Have you become a little deaf to the call of God on your life?

EPILOGUE:
WHAT **NEXT?**

Ask anyone who has ever tried to teach a five-year-old how to ride a bike, a teenager how to drive a car or an octogenarian how to access their email, and the chances are that they'll tell you that some of the hardest people to teach are the ones that think they know it already.

When we forget that we are eternal students, life gets a whole lot harder.

Right up to the very end, life continues to be a mix of learning and teaching, of receiving and giving.

The people you have just met know this truth well. They know that without being able to receive from God, they would have nothing to give of themselves.

The invitation

In Matthew 10 Jesus gives his disciples a special command: he tells them to leave him and 'heal those who are ill, raise the dead, cleanse those who have leprosy, drive out demons.' The full stop at the end of 'demons' is not the end of the matter, and neither the verse nor the command is quite finished. Jesus keeps on talking, offering a perfect explanation of why his disciples are being sent out in such a way: 'Freely you have received; freely give.'
(v. 8, NIVUK)

Scripture records this conversation in great detail, making it clear that every one of the 12 disciples is given this special task by Jesus. Even Peter, who soon will deny him. Even Judas, who soon will betray him.

The generosity of Jesus has nothing to do with us and our own merit. It has everything to do with him.

John records a similar incident that takes place later on. While his followers are in mourning, Jesus appears among them, showing his hands and side. They are overjoyed, says John, but the story does not end there.

'Again Jesus said, "Peace be with you! As the Father has sent me, I am sending you." And with that he breathed on them and said, "Receive the Holy Spirit. If you forgive anyone's sins, their sins are forgiven; if you do not forgive them, they are not forgiven."'
(John 20:21–23)

Jesus was sent and so the disciples are sent too. They are forgiven, and so they must forgive others too. He describes a never-ending cycle of relationship with God the Father, of receiving and giving forgiveness, of coming to the Father and being sent out to the world. Picture Jesus breathing on his disciples and it's not hard to imagine that he offered more than just one exhalation. Picture him standing by them, breathing in and breathing out.

Receiving God's gifts is not a one-off, static process. It is a continual cycle, intrinsically linked to our giving out. We receive and respond just as we inhale and exhale, much as we ingest and grow.

And that is the very heart of what it means to be a generous Christian. We give because we receive; again and again and again.

Donating vs giving

The perpetual nature of generosity sets it apart from the simple act of donating something. Donations cost us little, and merely use up the change in our pocket. They are not sacrificial, they don't require us to pause and count the cost, and they don't force us to lean on God to receive from him.

But donations have their place. The act of spontaneous giving, the habit of being open to the needs of others and being prepared to help those we might usually not have a connection with; these are all important elements of being generous.

Whether you're taking your first steps in your journey of generosity, or whether you're embracing the risk and already understand the value of planned giving, we hope that having read this book you'll know that generosity is about so much more than the money.

You might already know that generosity can be costly, and you might even know that it can transform you entirely. Perhaps you're desperate to see how infectious it can be or how it can improve your character. Maybe you know it's messy, but hope it will clear things up, or that it will change your life dramatically. Perhaps you just want it to lead you on to a wholly new destination.

Wherever you are on your journey of generosity, and regardless of whether you're rich or poor, employed or unemployed, homeowner or renter, retired grandparent or full-time Christian worker, if you know that you have accepted God's love and forgiveness, you will know that you have been given much more than you deserve.

And we hope that you will be able to insert your name into the words that Jesus spoke to his disciples: 'Freely you have received, ____________; freely give.'

What next?

Over the page you'll find details of the way in which Stewardship can help you continue in your journey. Opening a Stewardship Giving Account isn't a one-off act that will instantly transform you into a generous saint. Instead it is a small step towards a lifestyle where generosity is given the space it needs in your life.

By planning your giving, connecting with a community of similarly generous Christians and using the resources we'll share with you through the year, you'll be saying 'yes' to the invitation to give as well as to receive.

So join us and enjoy the adventure that awaits.

Take the next step towards making generosity and giving part of your lifestyle – open a Stewardship Giving Account.

We make it really easy and convenient to give:

1. We have **19,000** charitable causes, both Christian and secular at your fingertips

2. Besides supporting churches and charities, you can also donate to individuals working or studying for full-time Christian work

3. You can set up your account using a credit/debit card, Direct Debit or cheque

4. We automatically claim the Gift Aid on your donation, **adding 25p to every £1 you give**

5. No forms, no phone calls, no fuss. You can manage your account on the go and join us online. **Get set up to start giving in less than 5 minutes**

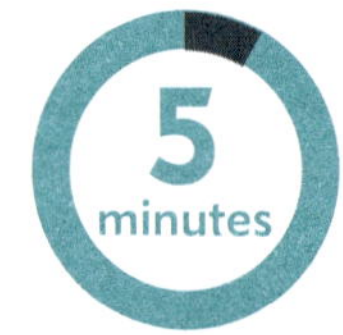

Go to stewardship.org.uk and click on the button

About Stewardship

Since 1906 we've been helping the Christian community in the UK to give and receive.

We love making giving easy and help over 25,000 individuals to give around £60 million each year to our database of over 19,000 charitable causes

We are committed to strengthening Christian causes, by offering practical, tailored support to help Churches and Christian charities to transform the world

And we inspire greater generosity through our wealth of resources, courses and campaigns, for individuals and churches alike, including the award-winning 40acts

To join a community of like-minded generous Christians, stay in touch and be inspired with more generous stories, lifestyle pieces and biblical reflections:

stewardship.org.uk

 /stewardship  @stewardshipnews